John S. McClung

Pray for the Kingdom

John S. McClung

Pray for the Kingdom

ISBN/EAN: 9783337170257

Printed in Europe, USA, Canada, Australia, Japan

Cover: Foto ©Lupo / pixelio.de

More available books at **www.hansebooks.com**

Pray For The Kingdom,

OR, THOUGHTS ON

"THY KINGDOM COME."

BY

REV. JOHN S. McCLUNG,

WICHITA, KANSAS.

"Pray For the Peace of Jerusalem."—Ps. 122: 6.

PRESS OF THE MIRROR,
WICHITA, KANSAS.
1895.

COPYRIGHTED
BY
JOHN S. McCLUNG,
1895.

Single copies sent postage paid, 25 cents. Five copies se! postpaid to one address, $1,00. When pastors, or others, ord· twenty or more copies sent in one package, they to pay carriag 15 cents each. The cash must accompany all orders. Usual rat to dealers. Write names and directions plainly. Address, Re J. S. McClung, Wichita, Kansas.

CONTENTS.

CHAPTER I.
The Dependence of the Gospel for Success on Prayer.

CHAPTER II.
Bible Exhortations to Constancy In Prayer.

CHAPTER III.
All Christians Should Learn to Pray.

CHAPTER IV.
Conditions of Successful Prayer.

CHAPTER V.
What Prayer Can Accomplish.

CHAPTER VI.
Further Illustrations of the Results of Prayer.

CHAPTER VII.
For What Shall We Pray?

CHAPTER VIII.
For What Shall We Pray?—Continued.

CHAPTER IX.
Personal Responsibility.

CHAPTER X.
Obstacles in the Way.

CHAPTER XI.
Young People's Societies and the Coming of the Kingdom.

CHAPTER XII.
Will You Not Pray for the Kingdom?

the kingdom than at the family altar. There is something so beautiful, so touching, in the entire circle joining in fervent prayer for the spread of the gospel and for the salvation of the perishing. But alas! this is a sight too seldom witnessed in these latter days. In so many Christian homes the family altar has been broken down; in so many others it was never erected. How much better and deeper the religious influence upon all connected with the family when the incense of morning and evening prayer ascends in the home. Here is something that demands the utmost diligence of pastors.

Before parting with my readers I desire to make two requests. One is, that they may overlook the literary and other defects of this little volume. The other, that all who read it may earnestly pray that the Lord may bless the reading of these pages to stimulating His people to greater prayerfulness and to greater activity in the service of Christ.

JOHN S. McCLUNG.

WICHITA, KANSAS,
August 6, 1895.

PRAY FOR THE KINGDOM.

CHAPTER 1.

THE DEPENDENCE OF THE GOSPEL FOR SUCCESS ON PRAYER.

"THY KINGDOM COME."

THE form of prayer which our Lord taught his disciples has been universally admired; so beautiful, so brief, yet so comprehensive. It gives utterance to all the needs of humanity; while it embraces all that pertains to the kingdom of God. And it should never be forgotten that the first petition in this summary is prayer for the kingdom; teaching by implication that our first and most important prayers should be for the prosperity of Zion. Hence if we follow the instructions of the dear Master, we will plead first and above all for the building up of his kingdom.

But this is not the way we usually do; we are apt to ask for almost everything else, then we may, in a few sentences, pray for "The peace of Jerusalem." In so many public prayers, at least, intercession for the success of the Lord's work is left away in the background. It has been remarked that some of the most noted preachers of our land in their public prayers do not mention sacred or religious interests, outside of those of their own churches. Often, too, in prayer meetings the petitions do not take a much wider range. But this is not as it should be. We should feel the deepest concern for the welfare of the Redeemer's kingdom in all the earth. Our interest in His cause should not be limited by the narrow boundaries of our church community, but our hearts should go out toward "the regions beyond." This we must do if we tenderly remember and faithfully obey the command of our Saviour.

And the object of these pages is to try and stir up God's people to greater prayerfulness in behalf of Zion. I want to influence His people, as far as in me lies, to plead importunately, to wrestle mightily with the God of Jacob for the advancement of his kingdom. May His divine blessing abundantly rest upon the effort.

And at the very beginning of this little book, in which Christians are so earnestly entreated to give themselves unto prayer, it will be well to notice an inference that may be drawn. Persons might suppose the author considered that prayer was everything; that it was all that is necessary to advance the kingdom of God. But he begs leave to assure his readers that this treatise is not built upon one idea; but that while the attention is turned to one great means of advancing the kingdom, still other agencies are by no means overlooked. The cause of Christ cannot be built up without active effort. The gospel must be preached; the word of life must be given to dying men. Without this, prayer is in vain. Just so, we cannot content ourselves by praying without giving of our means, without making sacrifices for our holy religion. Praying without paying will not convert the world. These means of grace are all necessary; they must be employed to accomplish the Lord's work.

But this book is based on the assumption that at this age of the church, prayer is not keeping pace with the other agencies employed; is not offered in due proportion. Hence so many efforts are without avail; the power is lacking, so that there are not the results there should be from the agencies used. More prayer is needed to secure divine efficiency and grander results. And one reason, no doubt, why more prayer is not offered is because the connections between it and the coming of the kingdom is not fully understood. The importance, the absolute necessity of prayer is not realized. Christians in general appear to think that it is well to pray for the success of the gospel; that this sacred duty should not be neglected; yet few seem to comprehend the fact that we cannot expect any gracious results without prayer.

But this is the case, for the gospel, of itself, is powerless; the truth of itself cannot change the hearts and lives of men. It makes no difference how earnestly the gospel may be preached, how forcibly the truth may be presented, this alone cannot bring men into the kingdom. "Not by might, nor by power, but by my Spirit, saith the Lord of Hosts."

"Without me ye can do nothing." The word needs to be accompanied, as at Pentecost, by the power of the Holy Ghost; as at Corinth, "In demonstration of the Spirit and of power," or as at Thessolonica, "Our gospel came not unto you in word only, but also in power and in the Holy Ghost." And when the divine Spirit accompanies the word, producing conviction and conversion, it is in answer to prayer. He does not come unbidden, unsought. He does not visit churches and communities in saving power without being entreated. The Father bestows his Spirit upon those "who ask him." When the Holy Spirit descends, bringing the blessings of salvation, we may not know who, but some have been praying. It is true that the Lord loves the souls of men; loved them so as to provide a most costly redemption, and now his great, compassionate heart yearns to save. Yet for all this he "will be inquired of by the house of Israel, to do it for them." "Ask and ye shall receive, seek and ye shall find;" these are the only conditions on which success is promised.

Of course we must not overlook nor undervalue the intercession of our great High Priest, still if prayer is not offered we have no reason to expect the cause of Christ to make any advance, or that sinners will be brought to the Saviour. It is like this: There may be a locomotive, complete in all its parts, still that perfect machine can accomplish nothing till steam gives it power. So in the Lord's work the most earnest efforts may be put forth, yet there may be no results, because the power of the Holy Spirit, which comes in answer to prayer, is lacking. Hence if earnest cries do not ascend to Israel's God, if there are no earnest wrestlings, the most faithful work cannot be expected to produce any results.

Turn to Paul's epistles and see how he implores Christians to pray for him. "Brethren, pray for us." "Praying always, with all prayer and supplications in the Spirit....and for me." "Finally, brethren, pray for us, that the word of the Lord may have free course and be glorified." With such burning words as these, he entreated the prayers of others on his behalf. He seemed assured that he could be successful in his work only in answer to prayer. And if he, the great inspired apostle, was thus dependent for results on the prayers of others, how much more are the Lord's servants now dependent for success on the prayers of others in their behalf.

Here, doubtless, is the reason why there is such a wide difference in the success of the same minister in different fields of labor. At times a man has had remarkable success; there is almost a constant revival, and all the lines of church work move on splendidly. On the strength of his reputation he is called to another charge. But how are the mighty fallen! Here his labors are fruitless and he utterly fails. Often the true explanation, no doubt is, one was a prayerful people, while the other was not. Would that it could be impressed upon Christians—burnt into them, that the prosperity of Zion depends on the prayers offered in her behalf. For then far more of those who really regard her welfare would be almost chained to their knees in earnest, wrestling prayer for her at the throne of grace.

CHAPTER II.

BIBLE EXHORTATIONS TO CONSTANCY IN PRAYER.

AS these pages will be occupied so largely in urging Christians to constancy in prayer, it will be well to show Scripture authority for this. To most people this might seem unnecessary, but this is a strange world, and there are some who seem to be afraid of people being too prayerful. They do not deem it wise to press the matter of devoting a good portion of the time to prayer. Religious newspapers have refused to publish articles that exhorted to greater devotion in prayer, yet their columns were open to almost any other contributions from the same pen. But it is easy to show that there is not much danger of going beyond the exhortations and the examples of the word.

Our Saviour spoke a parable "To this end, that men ought always to pray and not to faint." If we follow the example of the poor widow who is here commended we will come with importunity before the Lord. If our petitions are not granted at once, we will press our suit. We also have the example of the Man of sorrows himself. When upon earth he spent much of his time in prayer. We are told how he often retired alone to pray; sometimes rising a great while before day, or going out into a mountain and continuing "all night in prayer unto God." The old patriarch wrestled the whole night, till the breaking of the day, and still refused to let go without the blessing. The Psalmist declares. "Evening, morning, and at noon will I pray and cry aloud." "At midnight will I arise and give thanks unto thee because of thy righteous judgments." "But I give myself unto prayer'' There, too was "Anna, a prophetess," that honored handmaid of the Lord, she "departed not from the temple, but served God with fastings and prayers night and day." When Herod cast Peter into prison, "Prayer was made without ceasing of the church unto God for him." Then when we get over to Paul's epistles he commands in the most unmistakable language to give ourselves to prayer.

As "Pray without ceasing," "Continuing instant in prayer," "Praying always, with all prayer and supplication in the Spirit," "Continue in prayer." Thus the call to unceasing prayer rings out clear and distinct all through the word.

It is plain to be seen, then, that there is no danger of going beyond the precepts of the Bible in this respect. We cannot give too much of our lives to prayer. And I want to exert what influence I can in this little book, to induce Christians to give more of their time to prayer. I do want that they should plead more earnestly, more importunately, "Thy kingdom come." More of God's people should make prayer to a greater extent the occupation of their lives. This should be their business, the main thing to which their life is really devoted. In the morning begin to pray; as the hours pass by continue in prayer, and so week by week and year by year. It is not meant by this that the person cannot engage in some occupation, for a person can ardently pursue his calling yet give his days to prayer. We are not to suppose that we can engage in prayer only when we take time and kneel down. It should be clearly understood that acceptable prayer can be offered at any time, and in any place. While lying on the bed awake at night, while walking or riding along the road, or while the hands are busily employed in daily toil. Whenever the mind is free to think and the lips to move, then acceptable prayer can ascend. Some have the sweetest seasons of communion with God while they are most busily engaged at work.

The impressions will remain with me to my death that were made in my youth by reading an account of "The Praying Reaper." It was before the days of modern machinery, when they reaped the grain with a sickle. This man went out in the morning to reap, and he spent the whole day in prayer. He found at night he had reaped more than any day during the harvest, and it had been one of the happiest of his life. He always looked back to it as a day of Heaven upon earth. And who can tell what the prayers of that godly man accomplished that day? Were we faithful in improving our opportunities we could all have such days of Heaven upon earth.

But let no one imagine that because we can pray acceptably while busy at work, that this will suffice, and that hence we need not take any time for prayer. The Lord cannot be put off in that manner. It is a difficult matter to cheat the Almighty. If we are not willing to give some of our time to devotion the Lord is likely to reject that which we offer during our working hours.

If we want to give our time to the Lord in the way that will be most useful, we cannot do better than to spend it in prayer. It is prayer that moves the Lord to exert his power to advance his kingdom; this is according to the method of his administration. He has given prayer that prominent place; constituted it the great agency for building up his cause on the earth. Since this is the case there is little danger of spending too much time at the throne of grace. There is something very touching in the life of the late Dr. Bonar. He had always been a man of prayer, but as the years rolled by his seasons of devotion lengthened, so that in his later years that venerable man was not satisfied unless he had spent from three to six hours in prayer, out of the twenty-four. And while his ministry was wonderfully successful, yet eternity may reveal that he accomplished more for the kingdom of God by his prayers than he did in any other way.

Some might suppose that a life of prayer must be somewhat gloomy. That it would to some extent cast a dark shadow over the life. But nothing could be further from the truth. The one who gives his life to prayer dwells nearer, perhaps, than all others "In the secret place of the Most High; abiding under the shadow of the Almighty." This constancy in prayer keeps the person near to God, in harmony and sympathy with him. Thus his presence, favor and love are secured, so that the "Peace of God, that passeth all understanding," pervades the heart and life. Do we want to lead happy lives? We cannot render this as certain in any other way as by giving our lives to prayer.

A word of caution may here be in place, (though it is uncertain how often it might prove to be necessary,) agonizing prayer makes a greater drain upon the vital forces than the hardest mental labor. Prudence and good judgment should be exercised, lest the powers of endurance be overtaxed. Some by pleading too long and earnestly have brought on mental prostration. Care should be taken that we maintain our standing, in every respect, as wise, prudent Christians.

CHAPTER III.

ALL CHRISTIANS SHOULD LEARN TO PRAY.

MANY who read the title of this chapter will think it a blunder, or a contradiction. For, as they believe, all Christians, as a matter of course, do learn to pray. Would that all did; but it is a sad fact that there are too many prayerless Christians; that is, those who at least do not pray before others. Nearly every pastor knows this too well. In almost every church there are those who give evidence of piety, yet as far as taking part in prayer before others is concerned their lips are sealed; under no consideration can they be induced to make the attempt. Some of these, I am sorry to say, when closely questioned, have to admit that they are nearly, or quite, strangers to secret prayer. This is a mortifying fact, still there is scarcely a pastor, who has exercised fidelity on this point, but has found those among his people who are leading lives destitute of prayer.

One great reason why there are so many church members who will not pray before others, is that pastors do not urge this duty upon those received into the church, as they should. There is so much in getting started right, and if, when young people and others are received on profession, pastors should urge this duty upon them, the most of them would begin this duty. Then is the time to commence a life of prayer, and if neglected then it is so much harder to begin in after years. Still at whatever period in life people begin to pray, they usually find it hard at the commencement. There are scarcely any who do not find it a difficult task at first; perhaps they are ashamed that they cannot pray any better, and are discouraged. But the only way is to keep on and learn to pray by praying. Just as the case of a man who became noted in the history of our country.* He had been a member of the church for years, but had never taken part in prayer meeting. One Sabbath his pastor preached on the subject. After the sermon he told the pastor he was convinced that it was his duty to take part, and to call on him hereafter. So the next prayer meeting the pastor requested him to lead in prayer. He did wretchedly, however,

*Stonewall Jackson.

yet he said to the pastor: "I feel that it is my duty, and I want you to call on me." After a few attempts the pastor went to him and said kindly: "Perhaps I had better not call on you." But he persisted: "It is my duty, call on me." He blundered along and learned to pray, and the petitions that fell from his lips in later years were simply marvelous. He will be remembered for his prayers almost as much as for his brilliant deeds.

Let no one seek to excuse himself or herself from praying because it is hard. If this excuse were valid, as we have seen, then all would be exempt. We should faithfully meet this obligation, the same as any other. The way to look at it is, "It is my duty, and by the help of God I will keep on trying until I can pray." And in almost every case where a person is faithful it is not long before prayer becomes easy and affords the sweetest enjoyment. But whether it becomes easy and yields enjoyment or not, it is a sacred duty, and every Christian should learn to pray.

CHAPTER IV.

CONDITIONS OF SUCCESSFUL PRAYER.

IN order to pray acceptably and prevailingly for the coming of the kingdom several things are necessary. Only a few of these can be mentioned. One is a deep interest in the welfare of the church and of the souls of men. These interests need to be deeply, warmly cherished; they should lie very near the heart. We should bear something of the love for those precious interests that the Lord himself bears. We should have such a deep concern for the welfare of the church that we can cry with the Psalmist: "If I forget thee, O Jerusalem, let my right hand forget her cunning." And our hearts should be so burdened for the salvation of our fellow men that we can say with the apostle: "Brethren, my heart's desire and prayer to God for others is that they may be saved." "I have great heaviness and continual sorrow in my heart" for those on the way to ruin. Or with the weeping prophet: "O that my head were waters, and mine eyes a fountain of tears, that I might weep day and night for the slain of the daughters of my people." Our prayers will not amount to very much unless we do have something of this deep solicitude for the welfare of the church and for the souls of men.

We must also have an earnest desire for the coming of the kingdom. This naturally follows. If we feel a deep, heartfelt interest in the welfare of Zion, as a matter of course we must desire her prosperity. If our hearts are burthened for the salvation of the perishing, we will long to see them brought to Jesus. We will feel that we cannot endure it unless others secure eternal life. We need to get the welfare of the church and of the souls of men on our very heart of hearts; then with burthened, breaking hearts, we can but plead, "Thy kingdom come."

Again, if our prayers are going to avail anything we must seek to lead blameless lives before God and before our fellow men. If we lead inconsistent, unholy lives, no difference how earnestly we might plead in behalf of Zion the Lord would turn away and refuse to answer: "If I regard iniquity in my heart, the Lord will not hear me." Then if the unsaved see us leading inconsistent, wicked lives it turns them against religion. O how many professed Christians do such a world of harm by their manner of life. Ah, if we desire to advance the interests of the kingdom we must endeavor to walk very closely in the footsteps of the holy Saviour. "What manner of persons ought we to be in all holy conversation and godliness." Let not the frequenters of the theatre, the dance, the card table or the wine suppers; or the profane, the impure or the gambler imagine that their prayers are acceptable, and that thus they can help in the Lord's work.

No amount of prayer that such can offer can counterbalance the evil they are doing to their own souls and to the souls of others by their manner of life. Any such practices as these separate between us and our God, and cause him to hide his face from us that he will not hear. One reason, no doubt, why there are not greater results from the volume of prayer that does ascend, is that it takes so much prayer to counteract the bad effects of the inconsistent, unholy lives of so many church members. So much prayer is utterly neutralized. That is a hard statement, and would to God it were not true. When will the Israel of God come out fully from the world and be separate—a peculiar people? When will the car of salvation be freed of dead weights? If all who have named the name of Christ should lead holy, consecrated lives and would be as active in the Master's service as they should be and as prayerful; in a very few decades the whole world could be brought to Christ.

Only one thing more can be mentioned. We should not only pray; we should also put forth corresponding efforts for the upbuilding of the kingdom. "Faith without works is dead." Work, as well as prayer, is required to build up the cause of the Redeemer, and every one who wishes that cause well should improve every opportunity for active service. There may be instances where persons are so situated that they have no opportunity of rendering active service; under these circumstances prayer is the whole duty. But such cases are rare; generally when the prayer is earnestly offered: "Lord what wilt thou have me to do?" some line of usefulness will be opened.

It is too bad that there is such an amount of talent wrapped up in napkins in our churches; so much latent talent, so much capital unemployed, and hence that brings in no returns. So few, comparatively, engaged in Christian work. Many in our churches who are best fitted for usefulness do nothing. They seem to think that all they were brought into the kingdom for, was merely to be saved. They do not consider that the dear Master has any demand upon their time, their talents, and all that they have. Hence they simply fold their hands and try to get to Heaven just as easily as possible. There are church members of thirty or forty years standing who never yet have made any efforts to win others to Christ and to Heaven. It is to be feared that many in that bright world will wear "starless crowns." When will the drones be got to work? When can the latent talent and power in the churches be utilized?

At the same time there are a great many who complain and are deeply grieved because there is nothing for them to do. At times persons cannot find just the kind of work in which they wish to engage. All cannot be Sunday school teachers, or superintendents, or preachers; yet there are few, as has been said, who earnestly ask the Lord what he would have them do, and are willing to do what comes to their hands, but what they can find something in reach to do. And there is one line of effort and usefulness that is open for all; there is one department that is not overcrowded, and never will be; no Christian can ever excuse himself because there is nothing he can do—all can pray.

CHAPTER V.

What Prayer Can Accomplish.

HERE, perhaps, some are ready to say: "But we want a work that amounts to something; a line of effort by which we can accomplish visible, tangible results. If we merely pray how can we be certain that we have really ever done any good?"

No doubt many Christians sincerely think that it would be but little they could do through prayer; hence they do not feel to spend much time in pleading "Thy kingdom come;" while the facts are, perhaps, that there is no other line of effort that promises as large results; there is no other means by which we can accomplish as great and lasting good; nothing in which we can engage that really may do as much to advance the kingdom of God as prayer.

Yet it is a severe test of our faith, for in the nature of the case we can know so little of the results. Much of the prayer offered for the coming of the kingdom is of such a nature that nothing can ever be known of the answers. In other departments we can often see the direct results of our efforts; but we can never know in this life just how much our prayers have accomplished. We have simply to leave our prayers in the hands of a faithful Promiser. Our faith, however, should be strong enough so that we can confidently leave the case in his hands. And when "the mists have rolled away" no one will be disappointed at the results of his earnest wrestlings before the throne of grace.

For if a person was so situated that he should devote his entire lifetime to praying for the Kingdom, he would accomplish grander results than he could in any other way. Just devote the life to prayer, make that the daily occupation, the one business in which he engages, and no one need fear of being disappointed when he opens his eyes in eternity and sees the fruits of his life. Let me give a few examples of what persons have accomplished by their prayers:

A pastor had charge of a church forty years, and all through, those years were almost a continuous revival, precious souls in large numbers under his ministry kept coming to Christ. He did not know to what to attribute his success. At the end of those years one of the members of his church died. He never had been very prominent, but in securing information for the funeral services he learned that this brother had spent every Saturday night till twelve o'clock for the last forty years in praying for the blessing of God to rest upon the labors of his pastor the next day. When the pastor learned of those forty years of prayer in his behalf he knew very well where those forty years of revival came from.

Many years ago, in Virginia, there was a church in which religion was at a very low ebb. There had been no revival for a long time and the young people were growing up very irreligious. This greatly troubled an old grayheaded elder, and one Saturday night he went and knelt down on a bridge near the church and spent the whole night in prayer for the blessing to be sent. During the services in the church the next day a revival began which swept through that country. That old grayheaded man wrestled alone in prayer and prevailed. And often one person does wrestle alone with Israel's God and prevail; as in the following instance given by Prof. Charles G. Finney:

A pious man in western New York was sick with consumption. He was poor, and was sick for years. An unconverted merchant of the place used to kindly send him things for his comfort, or for his family. At length it occurred to him that the best return he could make for this kindness would be to pray for the man's salvation. He began to pray, his soul became enthused, and he was led on to a wider field. He knew some thirty churches and ministers, in whom he felt an interest. He set apart certain times to pray for a revival in their churches. He also selected some mission stations in foreign lands. He was very earnest in prayer; he was in such an agony of soul and he struggled so hard for the blessing that at times his family feared he would destroy his life. In his diary he would write that on such a day he was able to offer the prayer of faith, as he called it, for the out-pouring of the Spirit on such a church, and he trusted there would soon be a revival there. And the revivals came in very nearly the order he had noted that he had been enabled to offer the prayer of faith. These places included the mission stations in heathen lands and the place where he lived. This latter was a deep and widespread work of grace, during which the merchant was hopefully converted. It is within the bounds of truth to assert that there were few persons living at that time who accomplished more for the Lord than that hopeless invalid.

There was the case of another invalid, as related by Mr. Moody: A little cripple lay on her dying bed. She had given her heart to the Saviour, and she was distressed only because she could do nothing to secure the salvation of others. Her pastor visited her and hearing her complaint, told her that while lying on her sick bed she could pray for those she desired to be saved. He told her to write the names down and then to pray earnestly for them. He went away and thought no more of it.

Soon a deep religious interest sprung up in the place, and the churches became nightly crowded. The little cripple was eager to hear of the progress of the work and anxiously inquired the names of those converted. A few weeks later she died, and among a roll of papers that was found under her pillow was one bearing the names of fifty-six persons, every one of whom had been converted during the meetings. By each of the names was a little cross, by which the poor crippled saint had checked off the names as they had been reported to her.

One more case showing the possibilities of prayer must be given: The pastor of one of the leading churches in a large state, and an eminently successful "soul-winner," dates his success in the Master's work to the realization by himself and his people of the power of constant and united prayer. Up to that time he had been fairly successful in his ministry, but not more than ordinary. Since this baptism of prayer and of earnest labor came upon him, and largely through him upon his people, it can be justly said that there has been a constant revival. Multitudes have been gathered into the fold, and he has grown wonderfully in power and usefulness as a gospel preacher. What might not be accomplished if pastors, with their people generally, became baptized with this spirit of prayer? What gracious revivals could be recorded; what wonderful victories.

In view of these instances, and others like them that could be given, how groundless the fear that the seasons of prayer are wasted; that it is time thrown away. Who has accomplished more, in the same length of time, than those did in the examples just given? True we cannot always know the results of our prayers, but we can anchor our souls upon the promises of God, and confidently leave all in his hands. Many of God's dear people are doing this; relying upon the sure promises they are beseiging the throne of grace in behalf of Zion. But their prayers are so comprehensive, covering as they do almost every department of the broad field, that it is utterly impossible for them to determine when, where or how their petitions are answered. Yet their confidence is such that they sweetly rest on the faithfulness of Jehovah.

CHAPTER VI.

FURTHER ILLUSTRATIONS OF THE RESULTS OF PRAYER.

WERE it possible for us to know the real history of the Lord's work in all ages and in all places, we could easily see how the prosperity of the kingdom depends on prayer. But this we cannot fully know; so much of the church's history remains unwritten. As it is, however, many wonderful illustrations of the agency of prayer can be given. There was the day of Pentecost, when the Holy Ghost came in such overwhelming power, and three thousand were converted in one day. But the one hundred and twenty had tarried in Jerusalem pleading "the promise of the Father." They had held a ten days' prayer meeting and then the mighty power of God was displayed. It is safe, perhaps, to say, that if they had not thus waited upon God there would have been no Pentecost. Just so during all the history of the church from that till now, in almost every instance when the Holy Spirit has descended to turn men to God, the work of grace can be traced to special prayer.

As in Scotland, some centuries ago, a band of Christians spent the whole night in prayer. The next day at that place there were five hundred converts under one sermon by Mr. Livingstone. It was the same at Enfield where Jonathan Edwards preached his famous sermon from the text, "Their feet shall slide in due time." For months there had been most gracious revivals in that section, but the church at Enfield had not shared in "the showers of blessing," and they began to fear lest they should be passed by. So a number of the members met and spent all the night in prayer. During the delivery of the sermon the next day the Spirit came in wondrous power. The convictions of many were overwhelming; some crying out in terror, caught hold of the seats, really thinking that their feet were sliding into perdition.

The extensive revivals of modern times have nearly all been preceded and accompanied by special prayer. The sweeping revival of 1857 in this country was born in a prayer meeting. That deep and thorough work of grace in the north of Ireland in 1858 traced directly to special, wrestling prayer as its source. The same is true of the great awakening in Scotland the following year. There had been such extensive revivals in America and in Ireland, the brethren in Scotland yearned for a similar blessing to visit their churches. They agreed to pour out their hearts before God in prayer, and he was true to his promise.

There have been revivals of great power concerning which no record seems to have been left, as to whether they had been preceded by great prayerfulness or not. That in the southern states early in this century was such, when the Cumberland church began. And yet such revivals as these may have been prayed down. We have simply received no account of the matter. The prayers, too, may have been offered in distant lands.

Take the work of the leading evangelists at present; to a man they depend on prayer for their success. When they agree to hold a series of meetings at any place they arrange for special prayer services to be held weeks, often months before they go to begin their work. At times these men, when they have gone to the place and found a state of coldness and prayerlessness on the part of Christians, they have refused to go on with the work. They consider that to do so, under such circumstances, would be a waste of time, and utterly useless.

And these evangelists are nearly, if not all, men of great prayerfulness. They zealously devote all the time they possibly can to prayer. It would not be courteous to these brethren to invade their privacy by turning a search-light upon their seasons of devotion, but without mentioning names some of their habits in this respect may be given: Thirty years ago a young man was converted in a meeting held in one of our large cities by a man who had an international reputation. Under God he accomplished a wonderful work. This young man, from peculiar circumstances, spent a great deal of time with the evangelist, and he told me that they would hardly have reached their room when the evangelist would say, "Let us pray; let us lay these cases before the Lord." He said that the evangelist spent nearly the entire time between meetings in prayer. Years ago there was a man, not very widely known, but he was eminently a man of God, and was very successful in revival work. He was deaf—could not hear the ring of a bell or a rap on his door. The families where he was entertained during a meeting always knew where to find him when they wanted him to come to his meals—in his room on his knees in prayer.

It was my privilege once to participate in a meeting under the leadership of one whose labors it has pleased the Lord to bless above those of most of others; he has almost uniform success. After holding from three to six services during the day and evening, he would spend the most of his nights in prayer. Four to six in the morning frequently found him still on his knees, in his room, before God in prayer. If we should go on and notice the leading evangelists of former, as well as of modern times, we would find them, perhaps, to a man, eminent for prayer. They pay the price for success in their work.

Thus it has ever been; those who have accomplished great things for God have been men of prayer. Crushed almost with a sense of their own helplessness; deeply realizing "Without me ye can do nothing," they have been driven to God as their only refuge, and he has not failed them. "The eternal God is their refuge, and underneath are the everlasting arms." Had it not been for his prayers Martin Luther could not have set Europe on fire; but for his prayers John Knox could not have secured Scotland.

Then there is One before whose name all others pale, as stars before the sun—the blessed Christ. He came to do a work such as was never entrusted to another in the universe, and he, "the Man of sorrows," was pre-eminently a man of prayer. He laid the foundations of his kingdom in prayer, as well as in tears and blood. Glimpses are left of his habits in this respect; so often it is recorded he retired alone for prayer. At times he spent the whole night in prayer, "The morning star finding him where the evening star left him." If there had been a phonograph on these occasions when he wrestled with the Father, to have caught and transmitted those tearful petitions as they ascended for his church, what wonderful cries could be heard. Just such breathings, no doubt, as we find in the 17th of St. John. No one can doubt but that these prayers have been answered on during all the centuries, and will be answered to the end. But he prayed not merely while on earth; he has ascended to the right hand of God, "where he ever lives to make intercession." He is pleading now for his church, and is not his example one for all his people to imitate? How can they be his followers and fail to copy his example in this respect?

The testimony of the entire history of the church is that progress and prosperity depend on prayer. "Except the Lord build the house, they labor in vain that build it." In no line of Christian work can success be expected without earnest, importunate prayer.

In view of all this how is it that so many professed Christians are either almost or entirely prayerless, as far as the cause of the Redeemer is concerned? No difference how earnestly some pray for themselves they scarcely ever plead with God for the prosperity of Zion, or if their prayers ever do turn in this direction they are cold, dead, heartless. We often wonder, when we think of it, why the Lord does not make short work of it and speedily bring about the conversion of the whole world, yet when we reflect upon the prayerlessness of so many Christians, the wonder rather is that the kingdom of God advances as rapidly as it does. O, it is too bad that so few, comparatively, plead "Thy kingdom come." The tender command of our Saviour rests upon us thus to pray. There are such promises assuring us that the Lord will graciously hear and answer. Millions perishing yet in darkness and millions perishing from under the sound of the gospel appeal to them for their prayers. How can any of the Lord's people, in view of all this, refrain from prayer? What can drive them to their knees if all this does not?

CHAPTER VII.

For What Shall We Pray?

WHEN Christians attempt to pray for the upbuilding of the kingdom they are often at a loss to know for what to plead. And frequently when they have mentioned a few things they run out, and it seems to them there is nothing more to be said. Even when experienced Christians in prayer meeting pray for the cause of Christ, the poverty of their ideas is often surprising. But if any should devote themselves to a life of prayer they need not be at any loss for petitions to present. There are enough objects that tenderly appeal to our prayers to occupy all the hours of every day. When any attempt to present these objects, in all their phases, taking a survey to some extent of the wide field, new objects come crowding upon them; there appears to be no limit to the vast range of view. The field is the world, embracing every feature of the work and all the varied interests involved.

Look at it: There, for instance, are the Jews. They were once the chosen people, the seed of Abraham, the friend of God, the brethren of our Lord, as concerning the flesh. It is heart-rending to think of their condition, for they are still spurning the dear Saviour. Nineteen centuries after the advent of their Messiah they are still rejecting him through blind unbelief, and are going down to darkness and death without hope. How many generations more of that people are to perish ere they "look upon him whom they have pierced and mourn?" How long, O Lord, how long? We may be confident of this, if that volume of prayer was offered for them that should be, their eyes would soon be opened to behold in Jesus of Nazareth their long-expected Messiah. "All Israel" then would soon "be saved." There is no people that appeals more strongly and tenderly to our prayers than ancient Israel.

Again, take the present condition of Europe, and what spiritual desolations are witnessed there. In all those vast countries there is very little true piety. The teeming millions of that continent, to such an extent, are living in worldliness and sin; either rejecting religion altogether, or else satisfied with its mere empty forms. The religious condition of that country is dreadful, when we think of its millions hastening to ruin. Yet there are hopeful indications. The fields appear to be whitening for the harvest. Of late years there is a great demand for the word of God, and the Bible is being widely circulated. The Scriptures are in reach of a large portion of that people. Now if the Holy Spirit should descend to quicken the word; to bring the truth home to their conviction and conversion, millions in Europe could be brought to Christ. How God would be glorified and what a precious harvest of souls would be saved were those people turned to the Lord. How can Christians keep from praying for those perishing millions?

There, too, is Africa, that dark continent. The light is now penetrating its jungles and plains. Mission stations are not only dotting its shores, but also the far interior. Missionaries following in the track of Livingstone and Stanley have carried the gospel to the very heart of that almost inaccessible land. Oases are beginning to "make the wilderness and the solitary places glad." And many of the dark faces of that people are being lit up with the joy the gospel alone can bring. It is a very fruitful, hopeful mission field; there is a great readiness to receive the glad tidings of salvation, and if the Lord's people only remembered that benighted land in prayer as they should, "Ethopia would soon stretch out her hands unto God."

So, of almost every land. The outlook is hopeful in almost every quarter. The harvest of the world appears to be ripening; all seemingly that is needed to the gathering in of an immense harvest is the power of the Holy Ghost to bring the word home to the heart with saving power. And, let it be repeated, he comes in answer to prayer. How can the Lord's people neglect to pray for the perishing at such a time as this. O that every Christian would take to pleading with brokenness of heart, "Thy kingdom come," and "Come O Spirit, breathe upon these slain, that they may live." Were this course pursued, a scene resembling the last resurrection could be witnessed in nearly all the earth. For then the Holy Spirit would be "poured out on all flesh," and the dead in tresspasses and sins would be raised up to a new life. Immense armies would be raised up to serve the living God and "nations would be born in a day."

It seems clear that the great need of the kingdom of God today is a greater volume of prayer. Prayer has hardly kept pace with the aggressive work of the church. This is an age of great activity, and the work has been fruitful. Yet the gospel has been taken to such multitudes who have not embraced it. Millions upon millions in home and in heathen lands are perishing under the sound of the gospel, and from within reach of the Saviour's arms. Now, without stopping the sower, the reaper ought to catch nearer up. How can this be done? By greater prayerfulness on the part of God's people. For then the gospel, brought home to the heart by the divine Spirit, will be made "the power of God unto the salvation" of vast multitudes of these who are now rejecting it.

CHAPTER VIII.

FOR WHAT SHALL WE PRAY?—CONTINUED.

AS was said, when Christians are urged to pray for the coming of the kingdom, so many of them feel that there is really so little for which to pray, and their prayers are limited to a very few objects. Their attention has never been brought to survey the wide field, the broad expanse that lies spread out. The author wants to make these papers as helpful as possible, hence he will present some further suggestions as to the field our petitions may cover. This will be entirely unnecessary in the case of many, yet there are many who think the range is so narrow and circumscribed. It is so important to lead such out, and get them to gain some conception of the immensity of the field this petition of the Lord's prayer covers.

In making suggestions, then, let me say first of all, do not forget to thank God for what he has done; give him full credit. So often in our approaches to the throne we merely present petitions; we act as if the Lord had never enlarged Zion, sent a revival, or saved a soul. There should be more thanksgiving and praise, more expressions of gratitude in our prayers. There can be no doubt that if we were more thankful for the spiritual mercies bestowed we would have far more of these blessings for which to be thankful.

Of course our own personal interests are not to be overlooked; our needs, our friends, pastor, church, our country.

We should earnestly plead for the church at large; that Christians may have deep, fervent piety; that they may be built up in Christ, sound in the faith; that they may lead consistent, prayerful, consecrated, holy lives, active and useful in the Master's service.

That ministers may be holy men of God, full of faith and prayer, wonderfully anointed of the Holy Ghost; that they may have great wisdom and fidelity; that they may have an abiding sense of the sacredness of their calling, and of the eternal interests involved in their work; that they may preach a pure gospel, and be abundantly blessed in building up believers and in saving dying men,

That every means of grace may be blessed; that the word may everywhere be accompanied by divine power. Here I want to emphasize, the word is powerless of itself, only as it is followed by the Holy Spirit, can it prove "the wisdom and the power of God unto salvation." How God's people should plead then, if possible above everything else, that the gospel, however presented, may everywhere be attended by the convicting and converting power of the Holy Ghost. Want of prayer for the Holy Spirit is perhaps the great reason why so many efforts to win men to Christ are without avail.

We should plead earnestly for the children and youth, that they may be kept from snares, follies and all evil influences. That the schools may not be irreligious, tending to lead them astray. That they may early be brought into the fold, instructed and trained up in the service of God. That they may grow up intelligent, industrious, useful, prepared for the duties and responsibilities of the life here, and that to come.

That the Lord may choose young men who

shall preach the gospel, at home and abroad. That they may be thoroughly qualified and equipped for this great work. Also that He may select young women and prepare them to go as missionaries, teachers or physicians to the heathen.

That the gospel may be sent into all the earth, so that the untold millions who have never yet heard of Christ may soon learn the way of salvation. That the missionaries may be comforted and sustained in their work, and may have great success. That the heathen may readily receive the gospel, be rapidly converted. That the heathen converts may stand firm, be trained up for the service of Christ, and be prepared to go forth to others yet in darkness, learning the word of life. So that all the ends of the earth may soon hear and turn to the Lord.

That greater benevolence be given to the Lord's people; that they may give more largely of their means to spread and sustain the gospel. That all may appreciate what a sweet privilege it is to give, and that the treasuries of all benevolent enterprises and institutions may be abundantly supplied.

For the overthrow of intemperance, profanity, gambling, Sabbath-breaking, and all the sins and vices that hinder the success of the gospel and ruin the souls of men. For the destruction of Mohamedanism, Romanism, and all forms of false religion and of error, that deceive men and keep them from embracing the gospel of Christ. Where any special danger threatens the cause of Christ, that it may be averted. This is so often the case in foreign missions—as during the late China-Japan war; the present designs of the French against Madagascar, and the present (August, 1895) uprising against foreigners—especially the missionaries—in China.

For the speedy "binding" of Satan, and the removal of all hindrances to the success of the Lord's work. For the pouring out of the "Spirit on all flesh." For the triumph of the gospel in all lands, and the speedy conquest of the whole world to Christ.

Now these are but a few suggestions. This list might be enlarged almost indefinitely. Many will wonder why these topics were mentioned, while others of equal importance were not. "The field is the world," and it is not possible to cover the entire ground. It would be well for each one to make out a list of those things which weigh most heavily upon his heart, and that seem to him of greatest importance, and then bear these up before the Lord. In this vast sweep, different persons will usually be led out in different directions, so that by this wide range of prayer the entire field will be more nearly covered.

Would that the eternal welfare of our ruined humanity could be laid more heavily upon the hearts of God's dear people, so that they could not help crying to the Lord with tearful earnestness for our guilty world. Thank God this does rest as a heavy burden on many hearts, and it almost chains them to their knees. At times when some are bearing these precious interests before the Lord, the needs of our lost world start up before them with such startling vividness, that they are almost overwhelmed, and they can hardly bring themselves to cease from prayer. O that this number **were multiplied by the hundred.**

CHAPTER IX.

Personal Responsibility.

ONE great hindrance to the advancement of God's kingdom is that the great mass of Christians do not realize their individual responsibility. They are unwilling to recognize that any responsibility rests upon them, hence they are not ready to shoulder any of the burden of carrying on the Lord's work. They do not consider that they are personally under obligation to use their efforts to advance the cause of Christ and secure the salvation of their fellow-men. Thus the church is not awake. She does not come up to the help of the Lord. Too many are "at ease in Zion." Plead with them personally and try to get them to lay hold of the work and they are ready to say, "What is that to me?" "Am I my brother's keeper?" It is amazing that any who have a hope of eternal life can be indifferent to the eternal welfare of others, and unwilling to put forth efforts to save the perishing. It seems impossible that any of God's people could look with unconcern upon those around them—perhaps in their own family—going to ruin.

In the autumn of 1869 a steamer on the Mississipi river, heavily laden with precious human freight, took fire. In a little while the proud steamer was a sheet of flames. While all was terror and confusion, twelve men jumped into the yawl and made for the shore, though the boat would have carried forty or fifty persons as well. Having arrived safely on land, eleven of those men stubbornly refused to return to save others, though two hundred of their fellows were struggling in the river, ready to sink into a watery grave. Language fails to express our condemnation of such a course. They had escaped the dangers of fire and water unharmed, yet they would not make the least effort to save their fellow-men struggling there in the jaws of death.

But what shall be said of those who have been saved by the free grace of God, yet who will not do anything toward rescuing others. Having escaped the jaws of eternal death, their fellow-men perishing in sin around them have stronger claims upon them to put forth efforts to rescue them than those about to be destroyed by the billows of fire or water had upon those hard-hearted wretches, who coolly looked upon that scene of destruction. It is enough to make the heart sick to see the utter indifference of so many Christians in regard to the salvation of others. Those who neglect this sacred duty render themselves liable to be called to a fearful account before the bar of God.

The great reason why we should put forth our utmost efforts to secure the salvation of men, is because God is glorified in every soul that is saved. And if we are his people we are under the strongest obligations to do all we can to promote that glory; this is to be the ruling purpose of the new life. And there is nothing that brings such a tribute of glory to the God of Heaven as the salvation of guilty men. In redemption new attributes of the divine character are displayed, and all his perfections are made to shine forth with new luster. The divine power and wisdom are seen from the visible creation. "The heavens declare the glory of God and the firmanent showeth his handiwork." But the divine love and mercy—these tenderer characteristics—are manifested in redemption. Here alone we see the great heart of God—his boundless love, his infinite mercy. "Here the whole deity is known." No wonder the "angels desire to look into" these things, for here only, as far as we are informed, can they perceive certain traits of the deity. For, as far as we know, ours is the only race of fallen intelligences to which mercy has ever been shown. So that God is more honored in the salvation of one soul than in the creation of a world, because new and higher attributes are displayed in the scheme of saving mercy. All created intelligences will behold the redeemed of our race with greater admiration, with more rapturous praise, than all creation beside. To all eternity the redeemed will stand as so many monuments, commemorative of the divine love and mercy. And while eternity lasts, Jehovah will look with infinite satisfaction upon the redeemed, the work of all else nearest his heart. Redemption is his crowning work, his masterpiece. If then we have right affections toward God we must give ourselves earnestly to the work of saving men, which is the work uppermost in his mind and heart. In being zealous for the upbuilding of his kingdom we are zealous for his glory.

Then how we should feel for the unsaved! For it is such an awful thing for a soul to be lost. It is impossible for us to fully weigh eternal wretchedness; but O how dreadful to be banished forever from the presence of God; to have to dwell under his awful wrath against sin, a prey to fiery remorse; a companion of the damned from all worlds. And all this without one ray of hope for the future. That dreadful word "forever" is written upon the penalty of the law; upon the divine justice; over the entrance to the dark prison-house; upon the flames of hell. And shall we be indifferent to the fate of our fellow-creatures? Shall we look with unconcern upon the multitudes thronging the way to destruction and make no attempt to save them? When we are so aroused, when our fellows are in temporal danger, and will risk our lives even for their help, shall we be indifferent when they are in danger of eternal destruction? How can we ever appear insensible to their eternal interests?

Thank God some are alive to these great concerns; some are burdened for the eternal welfare of dying men. Such was Henry Martyn, of precious memory. Seemingly almost any position in the realm of Britian was open to him. He turned away from them all, and from one dearer to him than life, to bury his talents—as some look at it—as a missionary in India. After laboring there for years, without seeing scarcely any results, he cried: "I could bear to be torn limb from limb if I could but hear a Hindoo ask, 'What must I do to be saved?'"

This same all-consuming fire burned in the heart of a young man who sought appointment as a missionary. Said he to the Board of Missions: "Gentlemen, send me to Africa, send me to Africa. I know the climate is a deadly one, but if I can but die there I ask no more." And as he lay dying in that torrid clime, turning to his friends he said: "Never mind me; let thousands of us die, only let Africa be saved."

This passion for souls had possession of a Welsh preacher. "I am," said he, "a broken-hearted man. God has given me such a sight of the value of precious souls that I cannot live if they are not saved." This all-absorbing desire for the salvation of men is felt by thousands in the ministry. Ever before their eyes is a great throng rushing to destruction, and the query forces itself upon them, "What can I do to rescue them?" Often this feeling is so intense they can scarcely eat or sleep. Plenty of men, women and children in our churches have a yearning desire for the welfare of the unsaved. Their very "heart's desire and prayer to God" is that the perishing may be brought to Christ.

But the question is, how can this desire help but glow in the breasts of all Christians? When the glory of God is so intimately involved and the souls of men are beyond all value, why are not all believers pleading with burthened hearts for a display of his saving power everywhere? If Christians were only awake and on the alert! In a church or community where a few become burdened for souls and are crying to God for salvation, we say a revival has begun. Now should this become general throughout Christendom, if believers, the world over, were to become deeply concerned for the unsaved, and should wrestle on their behalf "with strong crying and tears," how the windows of Heaven would open; what mighty blessings would descend in all parts of the earth.

And how often the Beloved comes to his people while they are absorbed in worldly cares and pleasures, seeking to arouse them from their slumbers. He knocks tenderly, lovingly. His voice comes plaintively, "What, could ye not watch with me one hour?" He needs their prayers, their service, their influence. And there he stands knocking, pleading, "Till his head is filled with the dew, and his locks with the drops of the night." Yet multitudes of his people, in love with slumber, satisfied with their ease, resist all these tender appeals, and the dear Saviour has to turn weeping away. Dear reader has he thus been calling to you, and shall he call longer in vain?

And is not the Lord at the present time saying to the church universal, "Now it is high time to awake out of sleep." "Awake, awake, put on thy strength O Zion." But the only way for the church to awake is for the individual members to awake. That is the very thing I want to do; as far as I can secure the attention of God's people I want to say, "Brother, sister, you are personally responsible for the prosperity of the kingdom, and for the salvation of dying men. By the help of God rise clear up to your responsibility, so as to clear your skirts of the blood of all men." How can you bear the thought, my dear friend, of giving up your account at last to God, and of facing the unsaved within your influence then, unless you have endeavored, as far as you could, to bring them to Christ? Would that there were a trumpet that could as effectually waken slumbering Christians as the one that will be heard on the resurrection morning awakening the dead.

CHAPTER X.

Obstacles in the Way.

THERE have been frequent occasions for mentioning the difficulties in the way of building up the cause of the Redeemer. These obstacles may be divided into those that are preventable—as far as Christians are concerned—and those that are not preventable. It would not be profitable, perhaps, to notice those which are beyond our power to prevent, but I wish to consider some of the other class, so that they may be avoided. As far as in us lies, we should remove every obstacle out of the way of the advancement of the kingdom, and we should be extremely careful that we place none in the way. But too often Christians, by their conduct, do place hindrances in the way, thus perhaps preventing the answer to their most fervent prayers.

One great danger threatening the church of the future is that the Sabbath school children do not attend church. Nearly the only exception to this is where the parents live in the country, hence, on account of the conveyance, the children of necessity have to remain for church, but take it in towns and cities; at the close of the school a break is made for the door, and nearly every scholar leaves the house of God, to be seen there no more till time for school the next Sabbath. And so many of these scholars, when they get up in their teens, graduate from the Sunday school; then they are done with the church. Any number of people, with families growing up around them, seldom or never attend a place of worship. Speak to them about it, they will reply, "O yes, we used to attend Sunday school, but we were never accustomed to attend church."

Now, as far as Christian parents are concerned, this, to a great extent, can be remedied. It is their duty to see that their children go to church. While it is best, if possible, to avoid compulsion, if the proper course is pursued they can usually secure their attendance. In city churches some children have grown up and have never known anything else but to be at the church services. As a rule these early come to the Saviour and become pillars in the church. On the other hand those who have only gone to the Sabbath school, if they are converted they do not usually have a clear understanding of the gospel and of Christian duty, as they have not been accustomed to go to church, so often they are by no means regular in their attendance. So there is a great liability of their abandoning their profession, or at best plodding on, mere nominal members. Christian parents should endeavor by all means to correct this neglect of the sanctuary by their children. There is not a more beautiful sight, nor one more inspiring to the pastor, than to see the children at church.

Another danger is a disregard of the Sabbath. Religion cannot be maintained without the observance of the Sabbath, and the nearer the distinction is broken down between this and other days, the less power the religion of the Lord Jesus will exert. And this distinction in these latter days is becoming pretty well obliberated. I do not refer now to Sabbath desecration by the railroads, by Sunday excursions, concerts in the parks, base ball games, open saloons, etc., only in so far as Christians lend their influence and their patronage to these monstrous sins. I refer more particularly to the Sabbath desecration that has been creeping into Christian homes, such as doing marketing and other unnecessary work on the Sabbath; traveling on the Lord's day, especially on the trains; reading Sunday newspapers and other improper reading on the Sabbath.

This is not near the end of the list, but it is enough to show how Sabbath distinction is fading out; how the day is disregarded by many professors of religion. Here is a loud call for reform. It is astonishing how many members of churches will put off going a journey of business, pleasure or visiting until the Sabbath. We cannot say really that the Sunday trains and newspapers would have to stop if members of churches should withold their patronage, but it would be a serious loss to these institutions of iniquity. And it seems there ought to be piety and principle in the churches to stop a great deal of it. This profanation of the Lord's day by professed Christians is a reproach to religion, in the eyes of worldly people, and no doubt causes the Lord very often to refuse to bestow his blessing upon the church.

Then the almost constant change of pastors is a great hindrance to the Lord's work. It used to be that when a young man was settled in his first charge he was expected to spend his entire ministry there. But we, especially in the west, have fallen upon evil times, in this respect. The average length of the pastorate, in the denominations that choose their own pastors, is not much over two years. The pastor and his family hardly become acquainted with the people, so as to do efficient work, when they have to leave. There are many reasons for this sad state of affairs. One of the most common is a disposition on the part of so many church members to take up little, trivial things against the pastor. Often these are really not worthy of mention, yet they are brooded over, talked about, till the poor man has to leave. But so frequently in driving him away the church is split into two factions, and when the next man comes, one or the other is opposed to him, and soon fights him away. Thus a squabble is at times kept up from one generation to another.

And there is nothing that more effectually prevents the Lord's work than such strife. The Holy Spirit is grieved away and the people of the world are turned against the church and often to infidelity. When a pastor is settled every member who desires the welfare of the cause of Christ should accept the situation and do his utmost to make his work a success.

Sometimes, however, it is the pastor's fault. He is ambitious, restless or discouraged, so he tears himself away. And often the Lord whips him for it, just as he frequently does a clique in a church that unjustly turns the pastor away. Both pastor and people often see afterwards that it would have been better to have regarded that shrewd advice:

"'Tis better to endure the ills we have
Than fly to others that we know not of."

Or the advice of the apostle, "Be content with such things as ye have." Is there no way to stop this constant change, which entails such dreadful hardships upon the pastor and his family, and works such injury to the cause of Christ.

The tendency to ritualism is another danger now threatening the Protestant churches. This is a very insidious foe. It comes clothed in such an innocent garb and glides in so stealthily. But it is nevertheless a deadly foe to religion. The history of the church shows that it blights and destroys true piety. And it is so congenial to the human heart. We would so much rather pay our worship by mere forms and ceremonies than by sincere heart worship. But our Saviour declared "God is a Spirit, and they that worship him must worship him in spirit and in truth." The Almighty cannot be put off by a set of rites and ceremonies, however beautiful or aesthetic.

And there is no question, ritualism is creeping into our churches. Look at the way Christmas and Easter are observed, and Good Friday and other days are being taken up. Great strides have been taken in this direction during the last few years. If many of our fathers and mothers who went home to their rest only twenty or thirty years ago should return to earth and enter their old church on Easter morning they would perhaps exclaim, "What, am I in a Catholic church?" Now I do not say that this has gone so far as to be actually wrong, but the danger is, "Whereunto these things may grow." After the Arab's camel got his nose into the tent it was not long before he was clear in, and there was no room for anything else. It seems now that the camel of ritualism was getting his nose pretty well into some of our churches, and the sad havoc that ritualism has wrought in what was once pure, spiritual churches, ought to be a warning to all who desire a pure church to be maintained. The only safe way is to adhere to the old Latin adage, "Obsta principia," ("resist the first beginnings.") Don't let the destroyer get a foothold. Zealously maintain a simple, spiritual worship.

Still another danger that appears to be growing, is an inordinate selfishness. This is the natural tendency. As the country increases in wealth the love of pleasure and of luxury is liable to increase, and people are unwilling to make self-denials for the sake of Christ. I was startled lately by what a returned missionary said to me. He had been gone some ten years, and he said since his return he could notice that during that time a desire for self-indulgence and luxury had been growing among the churches, and an unwillingness to make sacrifices for the Master. He was fearful for the consequences upon the work of foreign missions. He may have been mistaken, yet it is evident that there is not that willingness to make any and every sacrifice for the dear Master, there should be. Christians are so far from reaching the example of him "Who though he was rich, yet for our sakes became poor."

And just in the degree that Christians are selfish; loving ease and luxury, and unwilling to make sacrifices, in that degree they are shorn of their power, consequently in the same degree the cause of the Redeemer must languish. There is an intimate and direct connection, in this respect, as cause and effect. Nor was there ever a time when the Lord's work demanded greater sacrifices than now; in wrestling prayer, in devoting time, effort and money to the work, and in giving self up to be wholly the Lord's. Why is it that all God's people cannot rise to the thought of the exalted privilege of making sacrifices for the precious Saviour and for the souls of men.

But I wish to speak more particularly of giving our means. What a crying need there is for money now, to carry on the Lord's work. What large and white fields, at home and abroad, cannot be improved for lack of means. In benighted lands many of the heathen, remote from mission stations, have learned something of the gospel, and of the blessed results of the work of the missionaries. And they often come long distances, pleading that missionaries may be sent to them. But, although there are applicants at home waiting to be sent to just such openings, yet these requests so often have to be denied for lack of funds. And how hard to refuse these pressing entreaties. There needs to be a revival, at present, on the line of benevolence. So many are unwilling to give of their abundance; others are unwilling to exercise economy and self-denial in order that they may be able to give; as a consequence the chariot wheels of salvation frequently move slowly, and precious souls have to perish in darkness, without a knowledge of the Saviour.

Will not every one give then, "As God has prospered him?" That is the standard, and it is certainly a reasonable one. And no person loses anything by giving. The Lord usually more than makes it up. Then, if we give from the right motive, we are "laying up treasures in Heaven," increasing our gracious and eternal reward. Besides, our money will do such good employed in the Lord's work; will bring such glory to our divine Christ, and will help to save undying souls. It seems wondrous strange that all Christians cannot rise to the appreciation of the "luxury of giving." It is a duty to give—yes, it is a sacred duty—but, O, my friend, it is a far sweeter privilege.

Here I want to address any of my readers to whom the Lord has given large wealth. There are many true Christians, in nearly all denominations, who, in the providence of God, have great possessions—some are millionaires. Brethren, one of the most desirable things in the world is to have large wealth, so as to be able to make large benefactions to worthy objects, and it thus affords such an opportunity of helping on the kingdom. But, brethren, it will be a fearful thing to meet our Judge if we have kept our talents selfishly hoarded up, instead of employing them in the Master's service. Large wealth brings increased responsibility, and may God deliver you from the awful fate of your money burning on your conscience like molten lava in the eternal world.

Meet your responsibilities, then, brethren. Give largely of your means to the cause of your Master, and thus be prepared to receive an approving verdict from your final Judge. "He is worthy." He has redeemed you with his own heart's blood, and has bestowed upon you all that you possess. Bring, then, your princely gifts and lay them at your Redeemer's feet. And bestow your gifts during your lifetime—at least a share of them—while you can be your own executor. It seems rather selfish to hold onto our money till we can hold no longer, then make provision for giving it to the Lord. Besides, when it is bequeathed, so often it never reaches its object—the lawyers get it. There is also such a satisfaction in knowing that our money is doing good while we are living.

One great reason why so many persons of large wealth do not give more largely is they feel that they must leave their fortune to their family and relatives. Now God forbid that I should advocate wronging the dear ones. They should be well cared for. Due provision should be made for them. That is but just and right. But let me remind the wealthy that they are under greater obligations to their Redeemer than to any earthly relations, and He, of all others, should not be wronged. And frequently the fortune that is left for the family does them no real good; it goes in legal contests; or if it does reach the family it really proves a curse to some of them.

In view of what constantly comes under observation, there can be no very strong inducements to bequeath large fortunes to relatives.

Oh that the Lord's people who have been entrusted with great wealth, or with only moderate means, may lay these things to heart, especially at this time, when there is such a crisis for funds to carry on the work. If some of our multi-millionaires would give a million or more dollars for the work of foreign missions, what an amount of good they could do. Funds are so needed for that work, and at present there are larger results, in the way of conversions, in proportion to the number of workers, in foreign than in work at home. And the pressure for money for the work at home is about as great. What an opportunity for people of wealth to come to the help of the Lord. This is an emergency that will determine whether the love of Christ or of self is stronger—a testing time. May the Lord open hearts to respond to humanity's need in such a way as to show the sweet, the all-constraining power of Jesus' love.

CHAPTER XI.

Young People's Societies and the Coming of the Kingdom.

THE "Christian Endeavor" and the other societies for young people are one of the most hopeful features of the church of the future. They wonderfully brighten the prospect for the spread of the gospel. These societies are doing such a work in helping and encouraging young converts, and in developing and training them for the Lord's service. This is a work that has always been needed, and it is curious that some method such as this had not been devised centuries ago. Every person is ready to ask, "How did the church manage to do so long without them?"

One of the best features of these societies is that they accustom the young people to take part in prayer. Young Christians need to learn to pray. They should be drawn out in prayer from their very entrance upon the new life. Unless they take up this duty then, they are apt to neglect it afterward. Now these societies come right in and tend to do this very thing, and the proportion of young people who take part in prayer now is vastly greater than it was during the last generation. Where these societies have done their work the situation in a church cannot be like one that was reported some years ago. There were some seventy or eighty members in the church, and of all that number only four or five would take part in the prayer meetings.

Not only so, the young people are now put to work; these societies get them right into the traces. They are thus trained for active service. Usually pastors now lean greatly upon their young people. When they want anything done they know just where to lay the hand upon the ones to do it.

Thus new blood and vigor are brought into almost every department of the Lord's work.

When we think back we are almost astonished that the churches accomplished as much as they did when there was so much latent power, useless material, such undeveloped sources. Since these energies have been awakened and this latent power brought into activity, her growth must be more rapid, her conquests must be greater. To me, the young people's societies is one of the grandest movements of modern times.

But while all this is true, I am profoundly convinced that, as yet, these societies, or at least many of them, are far from doing as efficient work as they should. There are "Dead flies in the ointment." As I have attended these societies, in different places, several defects in the method of conducting them have deeply impressed me. One of the most serious is the little time devoted to prayer. Not always, but so largely. Often there are only one or two brief prayers in the whole hour. Now this is not waiting upon the Lord for his blessing as they should. They should earnestly seek the divine blessing to rest down on all the varied interests.

Again, this affords little opportunity to draw those who need it out in prayer. And if the young people do not learn to pray i᎐ these societies they fail in a very import᎐ particular.

Then is so many instances there is a defect in the Bible study. The leader, perhaps, copies the references on slips; he takes these to the meeting, hands them around, and the members simply read these verses from the slips. Here there is no real study of the word. Even the leader did not search out references bearing on the topic, he merely copied them from some paper. The leader and every member ought to "Search the Scriptures" for passages bearing on every topic, and they should be able to give some thought which the passage contains.

Frequently, also, there is very little speaking in the meetings, and the young are not led out in this direction. Even on "consecration," or experience day nearly all content themselves by reading a verse. I have been surprised to see those who had been members of the church for years and ought to be able to to speak intelligently and with profit; yet they scarcely ever pretend to say a word. Now those who attend these meetings should gather ideas and learn to express them. If they do not, the society does not do the work it should.

But, as has been said, these societies, with their defects, have done a great work. They are training up and fitting the present generation for service, as no former one has ever been. They are an important factor in the future progress of the church. They possess almost untold possibilities for usefulness. And owing to the agency of these societies, I, for one at least, am looking forward for a more speedy and powerful coming of the kingdom of Christ.

Here let me beseech all young Christians who read these pages to lay themselves out in prayer for the upbuilding of the kingdom. Take a deep concern, young friends, in these great interests. Rest not satisfied until the welfare of Zion and of the souls of men weigh heavily upon your hearts. Endeavor to get into full sympathy with the dear Saviour in what he endured to provide redemption. You know the self-denial and the dreadful anguish it cost him. Try to attain something of that same love for perishing men, and a willingness to make any sacrifice to win them to Christ and to Heaven.

Also reflect much upon the worth of the soul, and what an awful thing it is for any to be lost. If these things lie tenderly on your hearts, the love of Christ and of the souls of men will constrain you to do all in your power to save men. O if these things are only impressed upon you, there will be no trouble about you praying for them. You could not help but pray. Pour out your very hearts in prayer for the perishing. Wrestle as long as you live in behalf of the dying. Thus only can your skirts be clear.

Remember, young friends, your responsibility; that to an extent you are accountable for the salvation of lost men. It will be a fearful thing when we stand before the bar of God, not to be able to say with the Apostle: "I am clear of the blood of all men." And if you begin to pray for the perishing in your early years and follow it up as long as you live, eternity only can reveal what your prayers have accomplished. When, also, you come to stand before the throne, you will have a crown studded with the brightest jewels to lay at your Redeemer's feet. And you will hear from his gracious lips the approval, "Well done, good and faithful servant." And in the eternal world many will come and thank you for being the means of their salvation.

What say you, young friends? Will you lead a life of prayer? Will you plead with brokenness of heart for the perishing, and do what you can by personal effort for their salvation? Or will you give the lost, occasion to complain, "No man cares for my soul?"

CHAPTER XII.

Will You Not Pray For The Kingdom.

IN VIEW, therefore, of the glory of God and the salvation of immortal souls, I do entreat all God's people to give themselves to lives of prayer. Brethren, plead as the days, months and years roll by for the upbuilding of the Redeemer's kingdom, and for the eternal welfare of dying men. The soul is so precious; such eternal interests are involved in the case of every human soul; it is such an awful thing for anyone to go down to darkness and death; yet what multitudes are perishing! As you consider the vast multitudes who have never heard of the way of life and are perishing in darkness, and the millions in Christian lands who enjoy the light, but are spurning the Saviour, how can you fail to plead that God may bring all men to a saving knowledge of the Lord Jesus? O, if all Christians only did this, how much more rapidly the kingdom of God would come, and how many more would be spared from dying "Without God and without hope!" Will not those in our churches especially, who are longing for something to do for the dear Master, take to pleading with all the heart "Thy Kingdom Come"?

And would that I could induce aged Christians to spend the remainder of their days in prayer. There are many aged ministers who have had to retire from active service; and there are other Christians who are regretting that their days of usefulness are past, and that all they can now do is to await the summons, "It is enough, come up higher." Yet if these worn out veterans should spend what remains to them of life in pleading for the coming of Christ's kingdom, they could accomplish more, perhaps, than in their days of active service. Thus their declining years might bear the most abundant fruit.

And would it not be a grand thing for all Christendom to observe a year of special prayer for the outpouring of the Holy Spirit in all the earth, and for the salvation of men? We are so inclined to do what everybody else is doing—even if it is praying—that if a twelve months were set apart for special prayer, so many more would join in earnest prayer. "The Week of Prayer" has secured the most gracious results; large harvests of precious souls have been gathered into the fold as the fruit of its observance. What grand results then might reasonably be expected if all the Lord's people, in all parts of the earth, were to spend a year in wrestling for the descent of the Holy Spirit, and for the salvation of the perishing? Could a year be thus sacredly observed, I believe under God it would secure the salvation of untold multitudes, and give a new impetus to the spreading abroad of the kingdom of God's dear Son over all the earth. The Lord's people never yet have proved him by prayer as they should. When will the sacramental hosts of God come up to their duty in this respect?

And there is an emergency on the church now that demands greater watchfulness and prayerfulness, because of new obstacles that have to be met. During the past, when the church had adopted new measures, secured better equipments, and thus been prepared for a more efficient, aggressive service, Satan has set himself to counteract these new agencies. Everyone knows full well that during the last two or three generations new methods and new machinery have been employed in the Lord's work, and this has been a period of wonderful activity and of surprising results. But the Prince of Darkness has not been asleep in the meantime, nor has he given up the cause as lost. He has set up new engines, adopted new tactics, and the church of today has to face some of the most difficult problems and meet some of the greatest obstacles of her entire history. If she is not girded with new force she will be worsted in the contest. Unless the mighty power of God undertakes in her behalf she will enter the new century in a crippled condition. Hence the providence of God and the welfare of the kingdom demand at present a higher standard of piety, a holier, more consecrated life, a greater degree of prayerfulness. I believe that through divine grace Christians will meet this demand, and that greater achievements await the church in the immediate future. But unless they do come up to the occasion wide-spread disaster and defeat may be expected.

Yes the prospect is hopeful, but it will be what WE make it. Would that we could come up to our possibilities. There is reason to believe from the word of God that a time is coming when our world shall receive a most gracious visitation from the presence of the Lord. A time when he will literally "Pour out his Spirit on all flesh," when upon all the world around there will be one universal revival. Millions upon millions will turn to the Lord, and "Nations will be born in a day." But we can be assured that that day will not come until a corresponding volume of prayer ascends for that wonderful blessing. It is perhaps within bounds to assert that the Christians of the present generation could bring about this glorious time, and secure these wonderful results. Brethren shall we do what we can to bring this about? Do we really desire that all the "ends of the earth should turn to the Lord?" And are we willing to pay our part of the price?

I must speak these burning words. They have been on my heart for years. I have also been trying in my humble way to observe this importunity in prayer. And I entreat ministers to dwell more earnestly on the duty of prayer, and to try and induce their people to plead more importunately for the enlargement of Zion. I do entreat every child of God who reads these pages, for the sake of the precious Christ who redeemed you, and for the sake of dying men, cry unto God with brokenness of heart for the building up of his kingdom and for the salvation of the lost. Wrestle mightily in prayer for the prosperity of the church, and for the eternal welfare of the perishing. And don't let your goodness be "As the morning cloud, and as the early dew," but persevere in prayer.

Shall the great multitudes go on to ruin and the love of Christ and the souls of men not impel us to plead for their salvation? Oh that the "Spirit of grace and of supplication" may be poured out more richly upon all God's dear people, so that they may cry more earnestly, more importunately "Thy kingdom come."

"Even So Come Lord Jesus."

www.ingramcontent.com/pod-product-compliance
Lightning Source LLC
Chambersburg PA
CBHW020300090426
42735CB00009B/1159